It's My State!

OHIO

The Buckeye State

Joyce Hart, Lisa M. Herrington, and Kerry Jones Waring

Cavendish Square

New York

Editorial Director: David McNamara
Editor: Fletcher Doyle
Copy Editor: Nathan Heidelberger
Art Director: Jeffrey Talbot
Designer: Alan Sliwinski
Production Assistant: Karol Szymczuk
Photo Research: J8 Media

OHIO
CONTENTS

State Tree: Ohio Buckeye

Ohio is nicknamed the Buckeye State because of its many buckeye trees. The buckeye tree got its name from the Iroquois, who noticed that the nutlike seeds of the fruit looked like the eyes of a buck (a male deer). The sports teams at Ohio State are known as the Buckeyes.

State Bird: Cardinal

Cardinals, once rare in Ohio, live throughout the state today. The cardinal was adopted as the state bird in 1933. The feathers of the male are usually red, while the female's feathers tend to be brown. A cardinal also has a distinctive tuft of feathers on the top of its head.

State Mammal: White-Tailed Deer

Although white-tailed deer are common throughout Ohio, most roam in the southeastern woodlands. They are the state's largest game animals. In 1988, the white-tailed deer was designated the state mammal. They have a horizontally split pupil that helps them see well at night.

State Insect: Ladybug

In 1975, the ladybug, officially known as the ladybird beetle, was named Ohio's state insect. At the time, legislators compared the ladybug's qualities to the people of Ohio. They called the ladybug "proud and friendly" and "extremely industrious." Gardeners appreciate ladybugs because they feed on insects that can harm crops.

State Reptile: Black Racer

The black racer snake, named the state reptile in 1995, can be found throughout Ohio. Because the black racer eats disease-carrying rodents that damage crops, it is known as the "farmer's friend." Some of these speedy hunters have been recorded going 10 miles per hour (16 kilometers per hour).

State Fruit: Tomato

Tomatoes are an important crop in Ohio, a leading producer of tomato products. Elementary school students worked to help pass the bill that made the tomato Ohio's official state fruit in 2009. Several kinds of tomato are grown in Ohio, including heirloom, plum, cherry, and yellow varieties.

The colorful lights of Cleveland are reflected in the Cuyahoga River near the Detroit Superior Bridge.

The Buckeye State

L ocated in the Midwest, Ohio is known as the Buckeye State. It gets its nickname from the many buckeye trees native to the area. Ohio is 40,861 square miles, which makes it a medium-size state. Ohio is divided into eighty-eight counties.

Ohio has rolling hills, flat plains, and sandy beaches. The eastern border of the state starts as rolling plateaus (raised land) and slowly settles into flat plains toward the west. The state's northern border is a long beachfront along Lake Erie. The majestic Ohio River cuts from east to west across Ohio's southern border.

How Ohio Was Formed

Massive sheets of ice called glaciers moved slowly across much of Ohio about fifteen thousand years ago, during the last Ice Age. The glaciers flattened hills, filled valleys, and made Ohio's four main land regions. Those regions are the Appalachian Plateau, the Bluegrass Region, the Till Plains, and the Lake

Ohio Borders	
North:	Lake Erie
	Michigan
South:	Kentucky
	West Virginia
East:	Pennsylvania
	West Virginia
West:	Indiana

A replica of a riverboat cruises the Ohio River in Cincinnati. The river runs along the southern border of the state.

Plains. As the glaciers melted, Lake Erie formed and then overflowed. The extra water eventually created a small stream, which grew over time and is now the Ohio River.

Underground streams in Ohio helped create caverns, or caves. In 1872, two boys, Peter Rutan and Henry Homer, discovered Seneca Caverns in Bellevue. Today, the caverns are a popular attraction for visitors to the area. Ohio Caverns, in West Liberty, were discovered in 1897. They are the largest caverns in Ohio, with more than 2 miles of known passageways.

The Appalachian Plateau

Most of the eastern half of Ohio is made up of the Appalachian Plateau. The northern part of this area contains rolling hills and valleys. The southern part of this area contains steep hills and deep valleys. It is not a farming area because the soil is not very fertile. Although forests once covered most of the state, many of them have been cut down. However, some of the largest remaining forests, such as Wayne National Forest, are still there today.

The Appalachian Plateau has mineral deposits, or areas where minerals such as coal are plentiful. Coal was first found in Jefferson County, on Ohio's eastern border. Since the discovery of coal, Ohio has become one of the biggest coal producers in the United States. Natural gas and oil are also found there.

The city of Marietta is on the southern part of the Appalachian Plateau. East Liverpool, famous for its pottery, is also situated on the Appalachian Plateau. Athens, Hocking, and Perry are some of the area's main coal-producing counties. Akron sits at the northern edge of the plateau. About two hundred thousand people live there, making it Ohio's fifth-largest city.

Sumac adds vibrant color in the fall to the Wayne National Forest, which is located on the Appalachian Plateau.

The Bluegrass Region

When someone hears the term "Bluegrass Region," they usually think of Kentucky. But this region includes Ohio, too. The Bluegrass Region (which is also called the Lexington Plain) is a small area in the southern part of Ohio. It contains rolling hills that are covered in a thin layer of fertile soil. Adams Lake is located in the Bluegrass Region. It is a popular recreation area where people enjoy boating and other activities. Shawnee State Forest, one of the largest forests in the state, is also in this region.

The Till Plains

The Till Plains, south of the Lake Plains, make up most of western Ohio. Both the highest and the lowest points in Ohio are located here. Campbell Hill, in Logan County, reaches 1,550 feet above sea level. It is the state's highest point. Ohio's lowest point is located in the southwestern part of the state near Cincinnati. It is only 455 feet above sea level. The hills of these plains are made up of soil and rocks that glaciers left there as they melted at the end of the last Ice Age. Most of this area was completely covered in woodlands before white settlers moved there and discovered the rich soil.

The Till Plains have the most fertile soil in Ohio. The region is where most of the state's farms are located. Farmers here grow wheat, corn, and soybeans. They also raise cattle. An area called the Corn Belt starts in the Till Plains and stretches west for hundreds of miles. It is called the Corn Belt because most of the corn in the United States is grown there.

OHIO ★ ★ ★ ★ ★
COUNTY MAP

POPULATION BY COUNTY

County	Population	County	Population	County	Population
Adams County	28,550	Hancock County	74,782	Paulding County	19,614
Allen County	106,331	Hardin County	32,058	Perry County	36,058
Ashland County	53,139	Harrison County	15,864	Pickaway County	55,698
Ashtabula County	101,497	Henry County	28,215	Pike County	28,709
Athens County	64,757	Highland County	43,589	Portage County	161,419
Auglaize County	45,949	Hocking County	29,380	Preble County	42,270
Belmont County	70,400	Holmes County	42,366	Putnam County	34,499
Brown County	44,846	Huron County	59,626	Richland County	124,475
Butler County	368,130	Jackson County	33,225	Ross County	78,064
Carroll County	28,836	Jefferson County	69,709	Sandusky County	60,944
Champaign County	40,097	Knox County	60,921	Scioto County	79,499
Clark County	138,333	Lake County	230,041	Seneca County	56,745
Clermont County	197,363	Lawrence County	62,450	Shelby County	49,423
Clinton County	42,040	Licking County	166,492	Stark County	375,586
Columbiana County	107,841	Logan County	45,858	Summit County	541,781
Coshocton County	36,901	Lorain County	301,356	Trumbull County	210,312
Crawford County	43,784	Lucas County	441,815	Tuscarawas County	92,582
Cuyahoga County	1,280,122	Madison County	43,435	Union County	52,300
Darke County	52,959	Mahoning County	238,823	Van Wert County	28,744
Defiance County	39,037	Marion County	66,501	Vinton County	13,435
Delaware County	174,214	Medina County	172,332	Warren County	212,693
Erie County	77,079	Meigs County	23,770	Washington County	61,778
Fairfield County	146,156	Mercer County	40,814	Wayne County	114,520
Fayette County	29,030	Miami County	102,506	Williams County	37,642
Franklin County	1,163,414	Monroe County	14,642	Wood County	125,488
Fulton County	42,698	Montgomery County	535,153	Wyandot County	22,615
Gallia County	30,934	Morgan County	15,054		
Geauga County	93,389	Morrow County	34,827		
Greene County	161,573	Muskingum County	86,074		
Guernsey County	40,087	Noble County	14,645		
Hamilton County	802,374	Ottawa County	41,428		

Source: US Bureau of the Census, 2010

Wheat, corn, and soybeans are grown in the fertile soil of the Till Plains. These plains cover most of western Ohio.

The rich soil may have brought many of the early white settlers, but in modern times, people come to Ohio for the large cities. Cincinnati is Ohio's third-largest city. About 297,000 people live there. It is located on the Till Plains. Dayton, the sixth-largest city, with about 141,000 people, is just a short drive north of Cincinnati. Columbus, the state's largest city and capital, is located in the center of the Till Plains. About 787,000 people live in Columbus.

The Lake Plains

The Lake Plains cover the entire northern part of Ohio. Many different kinds of fruits and vegetables grow on the region's fertile land. Most of the Lake Plains follows along the shore of Lake Erie.

Cleveland is the largest city in this area, with a population of about 397,000. Located on Lake Erie, Cleveland is a busy manufacturing and shipping center. Other cities in Ohio, such as Toledo and Lorain, also have ports on Lake Erie. These ports allow them to ship their products to other states and countries.

The Waterways

Thousands of years ago, Ohio was covered with water. Today there are tens of thousands of lakes and ponds, as well as many rivers and streams. The name "Ohio" comes from the

Iroquois word *O-hy-o*, meaning "great river." The Iroquois first used the word to describe the river, and it later became the state's name.

All the rivers and streams in the northern quarter of the state empty into Lake Erie. The other rivers drain into the Ohio River to the south. The major rivers in the state include the Ohio, Scioto, Miami, Sandusky, Huron, and Cuyahoga.

Lake Erie is Ohio's largest lake. Erie is the second-smallest Great Lake, after Lake Ontario, but Lake Erie is not that small. It is one of the largest freshwater lakes in the world. It is over 200 miles from east to west and 57 miles from north to south. Thousands of years ago, Lake Erie was much deeper. **Beach ridges**—sandy deposits that rise above the otherwise flat ground—can be seen in some spots in northwestern Ohio. These ridges show how high the lake waters used to be. Today, Lake Erie's deepest point measures only about 200 feet. Several small islands in Lake Erie—Kelleys Island and the three Bass Islands—are part of Ohio and are popular recreation areas.

Historic Flood

The greatest natural disaster in Ohio history happened in 1913, during an event called the Great Dayton Flood. The Miami River overflowed after a series of winter storms, and some parts of Dayton saw 20 feet [6 m] of flooding.

The Ohio River provided business opportunities that allowed Cincinnati to grow into an important city.

Cedar Point

Cincinnati Museum Center at Union Terminal

Franklin Park Conservatory

1. African Safari Wildlife Park

Visitors to this 100-acre (40.5-hectare) park in Port Clinton can drive through an authentic wild animal habitat, observing and feeding animals such as giraffes, buffaloes, and camels. There is a walkable area called Safari Junction.

2. Boonshoft Museum of Discovery

The Boonshoft Museum of Discovery is a children's museum and zoo in Dayton that features an extensive collection of both natural history artifacts and live animals. The museum is also home to a planetarium and observatory.

3. Cedar Point

Cedar Point is called "the Roller Coaster Capital of the World" and is the second-oldest operating amusement park in the United States. Visitors can enjoy the park's seventy-two rides, sixteen roller coasters, a beach, and an indoor water park.

4. Cincinnati Museum Center at Union Terminal

This unique-looking building operated as a railroad terminal for decades and has been used for many other purposes. Today it is home to museums, a library, and a theater, and is used as a rail station again.

5. Franklin Park Conservatory

Columbus's Franklin Park Conservatory was founded in 1852 as a site for the Franklin County Fair. Today, it is a leading site for **horticulture**—the study of plants—in Ohio and also a favorite location for weddings and other events.

OHIO ★ ★ ★ ★ ★

6. Hocking Hills State Park

Located in the southern portion of the state, Hocking Hills State Park is home to many notable rock formations, waterfalls, and gorges. With more than two hundred campsites, the park attracts Ohioans who enjoy the outdoors.

7. National Underground Railroad Freedom Center

This Cincinnati museum is devoted to the Underground Railroad, the trail taken by fugitives from slavery up through the Civil War. The center's larger mission is to educate and to support freedom for enslaved people around the world.

8. Rock and Roll Hall of Fame

People from around the world come to the shores of Lake Erie in Cleveland to visit the Rock and Roll Hall of Fame. Every year, the museum **inducts**, or adds, bands or solo musicians that have had a major impact on music.

9. Steamship William G. Mather Maritime Museum

This freighter ship used to transport materials such as ore and coal throughout the Great Lakes, earning it the nickname "the ship that built Cleveland." In 1990, the ship was reopened as a museum on Cleveland's North Coast Harbor.

10. Toledo Museum of Art

More than thirty thousand works are on display at the Toledo Museum of Art. The museum covers 4 acres (1.6 ha) and contains forty-five galleries, fifteen classroom studios, and a theater.

Hocking Hills State Park

National Underground Railroad Freedom Center

Rock and Roll Hall of Fame

The people who live in Ohio enjoy other lakes, too. Some of the major lakes in Ohio are Berlin Lake, Seneca Lake, C. J. Brown Reservoir, and Grand Lake St. Marys.

The Climate

Ohio's climate is about the same for all regions of the state. There are no tall mountain ranges in the state, which affects the climate in two important ways. First, there are no differences in altitude, or ground height. In places with mountains, there can be a wider range of temperatures. Second, there's nothing to block storms coming south from Canada or north from the Gulf of Mexico. A storm can blow all the way across Ohio with nothing standing in its way. Sometimes, strong weather systems bring very cold, very hot, or very stormy weather. Another factor affecting the state's climate is Lake Erie, which can make northern Ohio a bit colder in the spring. In the fall, though, temperatures along the lake will be a little bit warmer than in the rest of the state.

In January, Ohio usually stays around 28°F, which is just a little below freezing and perfect for snow. In July, the weather is warm and humid with an average temperature of 73°F. Ohioans spend the cold winter days snuggled in warm jackets and gloves from about

Winter temperatures all over Ohio create perfect conditions for snow to fall. The largest snowfall is near Lake Erie.

November until March. In the spring and summer, the days are warmer and stormier, with thunderstorms and even tornadoes possible. In the fall, the days are crisp and cool.

The wettest part of the state is located in the southwest around Wilmington. Toledo and Sandusky, in the north, have the least amount of rain and snow. People who live in northeastern Ohio see the most snow—almost 100 inches a year.

Ohio's lowest recorded temperature was –39°F, which was measured in 1899 in Milligan, near New Lexington. The highest temperature was 113°F, recorded in Gallipolis in 1934.

Wildlife

When the first white settlers arrived in Ohio, forests covered much of the state, but early settlers cleared many trees to make way for farms and towns. Today, forests cover about one-fourth of Ohio. Forest trees include buckeyes, sycamores, maples, and oaks.

Many different flowers and trees grow in Ohio's forests, plains, and fields. Some of these plants produce things people can eat. The shagbark hickory tree, for example, produces nuts. This hickory tree is also the source for delicious syrup. Native Americans used to make a refreshing drink from the berries of the red sumac shrub. A tree that produces a fruit called a pawpaw grows in the river valleys of Ohio. A pawpaw is similar to a banana. It is long and ripens to a brown color. In 2009, the pawpaw became the state's official native fruit.

The state is also home to a variety of animals. Different types of birds, such as cardinals, chickadees, and sparrows, fly through the Ohio skies and nest in fields and trees. Fish, amphibians, and other aquatic animals live in Ohio's lakes, rivers, and streams. Ohio has snakes, turtles, salamanders, and frogs. Many of its woodland animals are small. In the forests are woodland creatures such as white-tailed deer, raccoons, opossums, squirrels, bats, and rabbits. There were once many larger animals in Ohio's wilderness, such as wolves, cougars, bison, and elk. As more people moved into the area, the number of large wild animals decreased.

The black bear, for example, lived throughout the state at one time. By the 1850s, however, there were no black bears left in Ohio. Black bear populations are coming back because many areas of the state are regrowing the forests where black bears live. Scientists

The pawpaw, which grows in river valleys, is Ohio's official native fruit.

recently counted more than one hundred black bears in Ohio, and some of them were females with cubs.

Bald eagles are also making a comeback. In 1979, the state had only four nesting pairs. Today, it has more than two hundred. Bald eagles were **endangered** at one point. When a type of animal is considered endangered, it's because there are so few left that the animal could become extinct. The bald eagles in Ohio were endangered because of habitat loss and pesticides. Pesticides—chemicals that kill insects—eventually wash into the rivers and lakes and poison fish. Bald eagles eat the poisoned fish and get sick or die from the pesticides. Now many of the most dangerous pesticides are banned, so fish and bald eagles are are much healthier.

Like bald eagles, beavers were once plentiful in what is now Ohio. In the 1700s and early 1800s, however, trappers could earn a great deal of money selling beaver skins, and huge numbers of beavers were killed. By 1830, there were few beavers left. When beaver skins were no longer so popular, people stopped killing so many. The beaver population began to grow again. By the 1970s, it was estimated that more than five thousand beavers lived in Ohio. Scientists today believe that the beaver population has increased to more than twenty-five thousand.

Diverse Wildlife

Ohio's climate varies depending on your location in the state. As a result, you can find plants and animals in some parts of the state but not others. The common wall lizard, found often in Cincinnati, is one example of a subtropical animal that makes its home in the state.

Endangered Wildlife in Ohio

Ohio has several species of plants and animals that are considered endangered. Wildlife can be threatened by humans removing their habitats. Animals are also threatened by pesticides, overhunting, and pollution.

Several bird species, including the sandhill crane, the common tern, the golden-winged warbler, and the trumpeter

Efforts to help the trumpeter swan, the world's largest waterfowl, are bringing the birds back to Ohio.

swan, are on the state's list of endangered animals. The trumpeter swan is white with a black beak. It is the world's largest waterfowl. Trumpeter swans had almost disappeared by the early 1900s because they were hunted for food and feathers. By the mid 1900s, both the United States and Canada had programs to help restore them. In 1996, Ohio joined a group of states that raised trumpeter swans in zoos and released several pairs into the wild. Today, the state has about seventy pairs of trumpeter swans.

The list of endangered species in Ohio also includes mammals such as the Indiana bat, plants like the running buffalo clover, and insects such as the American burying beetle.

10 KEY PLANTS AND ANIMALS

1. Cicada

Many Ohioans call this insect a locust, but cicadas and locusts belong to different families of insects. The male cicada produces a mating call by vibrating its drumlike abdomen to attract females.

2. Jack-in-the-Pulpit

This uniquely named plant has large, glossy leaves and distinctive hooded flowers. In late summer, it sprouts a cluster of bright red berries. The plant is considered a tuber and can be eaten if dried or cooked.

3. Little Brown Bat

The little brown bat is one of thirteen bat species found in Ohio. Recently, the population of this bat has declined, causing them to be placed on a list of "species of concern." State officials are investigating the decline.

4. Perch

The yellow perch, native to Ohio, can be found in lakes, ponds, and slow-moving rivers. This fish, which is golden yellow with black stripes, prefers clear water with a sandy bottom. It is also known as lake or raccoon perch.

5. Persimmon Tree

Native to Ohio, the persimmon tree grows in the southern part of the state. Because persimmon wood is very hard, it is used by businesses that produce wood heads for golf clubs and cue sticks for billiards.

Cicada

Jack-in-the-Pulpit

Little Brown Bat

6. Red-Tailed Hawk

These large birds have broad wings and a short, fan-shaped tail that helps them soar for long periods. Red-tailed hawks are not endangered, but it is illegal to hunt them because of their important role—controlling the number of small mammals—in the ecosystem.

Red-Tailed Hawk

7. Scarlet Carnation

Ohio native President William McKinley wore a carnation in his lapel for luck during his political career. After McKinley was assassinated in 1901, the Ohio legislature honored him by making the scarlet carnation the state flower in 1904.

8. Trillium

The trillium is Ohio's state wildflower. It has three large ruffled petals and three large oval leaves. Its name comes from the Latin word for "three." Trillium is found throughout Ohio in the early spring.

Scarlet Carnation

9. Weasel

Weasels live throughout the United States, but their numbers are especially high in Ohio. Weasels live in forests and on Ohio farmlands, as long as there is water nearby. Catching and eating mice is one of the weasel's specialties.

10. White Trout Lily

This plant is a perennial, meaning it returns every year. Each plant produces a single white flower with curved petals. The white trout lily can spread and produce large colonies if left undisturbed.

Weasel

The open mouth of a snake can be seen in this aerial view of Serpent Mound, which is 1,330 feet (405 m) long.

From the Beginning

2

Scientists and historians estimate that people have lived in what is now Ohio for about fifteen thousand years. The first people, called Paleo-Indians, inhabited Ohio during the last Ice Age. Paleo-Indians moved from place to place, hunting wild animals, fishing, and gathering fruits and nuts. They used **flint**, a type of hard rock found in the area, to make tools and weapons. "Paleo" means ancient.

Over time, the climate grew warmer and the glaciers melted. Thick forests began to grow. Like their Paleo-Indian ancestors, the Archaic people hunted and gathered food. Unlike the Paleo-Indians, however, they settled down in permanent camps. They, too, mined flint and other stones to make axes used to cut down trees, build canoes, and decorate their spears.

Mound Builders

The Woodland period started in today's Ohio about three thousand years ago. During this period, people began farming more than hunting and gathering. Prehistoric people started to settle into more permanent villages, create pottery, harvest crops, and build elaborate mounds with raised piles of earth and stone. The mounds were used to bury the dead and other treasures. They were often built in the shape of animals or other figures.

The first of these Woodland groups was the Adena. The Adena people were the area's first farmers. They grew crops such as squash and sunflowers. Because they needed to tend their various crops, the Adena people built small, permanent villages.

Serpent Mound is the largest mound in the United States. It is likely that the Fort Ancient people built it more than one thousand years ago. Serpent Mound is 1,330 feet long and looks like a huge snake. It has open jaws at one end.

Another Woodland group called the Hopewell lived in the area about 1,500 years ago. They built gigantic mounds around their hundreds of acres of land. The Hopewell lived in small villages where they grew crops, fished, hunted wild game, and gathered plants. They

Archaeologists use a screen to sift dirt in search of Native American artifacts at an excavation site in Chillicothe.

were also excellent traders. They obtained shells from the Gulf of Mexico, copper from the Great Lakes region, and a mineral called mica from the Carolinas. Many of the mounds built by the Hopewell have been found by archaeologists. They provide lots of information about the Hopewell culture. Burial mounds were found that gave historians clues about how their society was organized. The burial mounds at Chillicothe are some of the best examples of burial mounds. Archaeologists consider Ohio to be one of the most important locations for discoveries related to the Hopewell.

From 600 CE to 1200 CE, the culture began to change. Villages grew larger, and many communities built walls or ditches around their settlements to protect themselves. They began using bows and arrows for hunting and weapons. While the Woodland people still cultivated squash and sunflowers, they began to grow corn, or maize, around 800 CE. Some of the last groups to live in the area until the 1600s were the Fort Ancient people in southern Ohio and the Sandusky and Whittlesey peoples in the north.

The Iroquois

In the 1600s, the Iroquois people came to the region. They had left what is now New York to find better hunting grounds, and they found lots of wildlife and edible plants in the land that is now Ohio. They pushed out the other people who had lived in that region.

By the 1700s, as the Iroquois grew less powerful in what is now Ohio, other Native American groups began to move into the area. The Huron moved south from Canada and settled around the Sandusky River. Another Native American group, the Miami people, came from the west. They set up villages along the rivers that now have their name—the Great Miami and the Little Miami. Some Iroquois first moved to Ohio around this time. The Mingo were a small group of Native Americans related to the Iroquois. They left the Iroquois homeland in the New York area and settled mostly in eastern and central Ohio. The Lenape people, also called the Delaware, settled in eastern Ohio. The Shawnee, who were pushed out of Pennsylvania by white settlers, moved into southern Ohio.

French and English Control

Europeans began exploring the land that is now Ohio in the mid-1600s. A French explorer from Canada named René-Robert Cavelier, sieur de La Salle, was probably the first Eurpoean in what is now Ohio. La Salle is believed to have explored the Ohio River as early as 1669. France claimed the region, but England also thought it had a right to the land because it was next to the British colonies.

This engraving shows Native Americans meeting with French military leaders on the banks of the Muskingum River.

For the next century, the French and the English fought over the right to claim the land they called the Ohio Country. This region included most of what would become Ohio, as well as parts of Indiana, West Virginia, and Pennsylvania. Both the French and the English set up fur-trading companies in the region. Both wanted to control trading with the Native Americans. Both tried to convince different Native American groups to join them in their wars.

The Native People

This image of Tecumseh, chief of the Shawnee, was published in 1887.

Native Americans have played an important role in Ohio's cultural landscape for centuries. The original groups in the area were the Erie, Kickapoo, and Shawnee. Many groups from other regions were forced to migrate to Ohio after European settlers arrived on the continent. They were the Lenape (Delaware), Miami, Ottawa, Ohio Seneca, and Huron (Wyandot).

Most of the original Native people in the Ohio area spoke a version of the Algonquian language. They lived largely in permanent homes in villages, and their food source was based on farming. The kinds of houses they lived in were varied. Many lived in domed houses. The Miami lived in oval houses with walls made of woven reeds. They also hunted animals like deer using a bow and arrow, tomahawks, and spears. The Shawnee people were different, as they were a migratory people who lived in scattered villages across the region and moved frequently from place to place. Many Native Americans in this area wore clothing made out of animal hide. The men wore **breechcloths** and the women wore skirts and leggings. Beads and feathers were sometimes used to decorate clothing, especially items used for special occasions or ceremonies.

European settlers made an impact on Ohio's Native people before they even arrived in the region. When Native Americans from other areas were forced to move there, they brought European diseases like smallpox that **decimated**, or nearly wiped out, the Native population already living there. Most of the Native Americans who were living in the region originally either joined other groups or moved to different areas, including the southern portion of the United States, after the Europeans arrived. Most of the remaining Native Americans were forced to relocate during the 1800s.

Today, there are no federally recognized Native American nations in Ohio. The Native people are not gone, but most of them moved to other parts of the country. Many Ohio Native Americans, particularly those who were members of the Shawnee and Miami nations, moved to Oklahoma. There is still a small but proud group of Native Americans living in Oklahoma today.

Spotlight on the Shawnee

The name of the Shawnee people comes from the Shawnee word shawanwa, meaning "southerner."

Distribution: Most of the Shawnee people originally lived in Ohio, Kentucky, and Indiana. Their migratory status means that Shawnee people could once be found in places as far-flung as New York and Georgia. Today, most Shawnee live in Oklahoma.

Food: Like many other Native Americans in the region, the Shawnee were farmers. The women in the tribe were in charge of the farming and harvesting, and would raise corn, squash, beans, and other crops. Shawnee men hunted deer, turkeys, and other small animals in the forest. They also fished in rivers and lakes. Soups, stews, and cornbread were important dishes to the Shawnee.

Homes: The Shawnee lived in villages made up of small round houses called wigwams. Wigwams usually had wood frames and were covered in birch bark. Each village also had a larger council house made of wood where leaders could gather.

Clothes: Shawnee clothes were made of animal hide and other materials found in nature. Women wore skirts and leggings, and men wore breechcloths and leggings. In cold weather, both men and women wore ponchos to stay warm. Shawnee people wore moccasins on their feet. Some wore headbands decorated with beads and feathers.

Artwork: The Shawnee people were known for their beadwork, pottery, and woodcarving. They also made wampum, artwork featuring white and purple beads made from shells. The designs on wampum belts often told a story or represented a family's history.

The ongoing conflict between France and Great Britain ended with the French and Indian War (1754–1763). Britain won the war and the right to claim all of the Ohio Country (as well as almost all the rest of North America east of the Mississippi River).

The Northwest Territory

After Britain won the French and Indian War, it tried to keep American colonists from moving west into the Ohio Country. Britain wanted good relations with the region's Native American groups in order to avoid wars and protect its fur trade. Soon after, war broke out between the American colonists and Britain. During the American Revolution (1775–1783), the American colonists fought for independence from Britain.

After the colonists won the American Revolution, the United States was formed, and Britain gave up its claim to the Ohio Country. The United States claimed the area northwest of the Ohio River and called it the Northwest Territory. This large area of frontier land included the present-day states of Ohio, Indiana, Illinois, Michigan, and

George Washington fought on the side of the British in the Ohio Country during the French and Indian War.

Wisconsin, as well as part of Minnesota.

On July 13, 1787, the Northwest Ordinance was passed. This document explained how the Northwest Territory was to be divided and governed. The Northwest Ordinance helped Ohio become the seventeenth state. According to the document, the US Congress selected the first governor. As soon as five thousand male landowners lived in the territory, they could elect their own representation in Congress. Later, when sixty thousand people lived in one portion of the territory, that portion could apply to become a state.

American settlers were eager to move into the Northwest Territory. In 1788, pioneers from New England founded Marietta. It was the first permanent settlement by people of European descent in the area. Marietta (named after France's Queen Marie Antoinette) was declared the first capital of the Northwest Territory. General Arthur St. Clair was named governor of the Northwest Territory.

Battle of Fallen Timbers

As more and more Americans from the East settled the Northwest Territory, the region's Native Americans fought to keep their land. After several victories, in 1794, they suffered a terrible defeat at the Battle of Fallen Timbers, near present-day Toledo. The area got its name from trees that had been knocked down by a tornado. General "Mad Anthony" Wayne led an army of three thousand troops in the battle. The Native American forces were led by a commander named Blue Jacket and made up of members of several Native American nations. When the United States forces got closer, the Native Americans escaped toward Fort Miami, which was British. The British soldiers were unwilling to help because they didn't want another war with the Americans. Native Americans signed the Treaty of Greenville in 1795. The treaty gave most of their lands in Ohio to the United States. When the British heard the Americans had won, they closed their forts in the area. General Wayne had new forts built for the Americans in what is now Toledo.

Making a Buckeye Wreath

Gather buckeyes from your neighborhood and hang this wreath in your home to show your Ohio pride. If you can't find buckeyes outside, try your local grocery or craft store. Chestnuts or horse chestnuts are very similar and can be used as well.

What You Need

A sturdy plastic plate or
    Styrofoam ring
Several (about 2–3 cups)
    buckeyes or chestnuts
Scissors
Glue (A hot glue gun works well;
    ask a grown-up for help)
Brown crepe paper (if using
    a ring)
Acorns, pine cones, walnuts, or
    leaves (optional)
Bows, glitter, yarn, paint, or other decorative items (optional)

What To Do

- Use the scissors to cut the inner circle out of the paper plate so you are left with a wreath shape. You may need a grown-up's help for this. Discard the inner circle part. If using a Styrofoam ring, wrap in brown crepe paper.
- Place a small amount of glue on each buckeye and glue it to the plate or ring. Place the buckeyes close together so you can't see the plate behind them.
- Continue until buckeyes cover as much of the plate as possible.
- Glue the pine cones, acorns, or leaves onto the wreath around the buckeyes to decorate it.
- Add the glitter, bow, paint or other decorative items in any way you like.
- Allow the wreath to sit for about 30 minutes so it dries completely.
- Once dry, display your wreath with pride! Ask an adult for help if you want to hang it on the wall.

Native Americans were forced to give up most of their land in Ohio after their defeat at the Battle of Fallen Timbers.

Statehood

By 1803, the eastern portion of the Northwest Territory had enough residents for Ohio to apply for statehood. On March 1, 1803, Ohio became the seventeenth US state. It was the first state made from land of the Northwest Territory.

Ohio's first capital was Chillicothe. Zanesville was made the capital in 1810, but two years later, the legislature returned the capital to Chillicothe. Then, in 1816, Columbus was chosen as Ohio's permanent state capital. The capital was named after explorer Christopher Columbus.

Moses Cleaveland of Connecticut founded Cleveland in 1796. According to one legend, the local newspaper at the time dropped the "a" from Cleaveland's name to fit it in a headline.

Native American Losses

Although Ohio was now a state, the relationship between white settlers and Native Americans was troubled. By the 1800s, many Native American groups were suffering. More and more of their land was being taken over by white settlers, and hunting for the fur trade meant that there were fewer animals in the area. Many Native Americans had trouble finding food.

Native American leaders were worried about their people and the loss of their land. Shawnee chief Tecumseh and his brother, known as the Prophet, tried to join many groups of Native Americans to stop white settlers from taking their land. General William Henry Harrison, who later

In Their Own Words

"It is easy to pronounce, is pleasant in sound, and there is no other city of that name on the American continent."
—Merchant Willard J. Daniels, on how Toledo was named

Shawnee chief Tecumseh died in battle while fighting to keep settlers from taking land from Native American tribes.

Tecumseh.

became president of the United States, knew of Tecumseh's plans. In 1811, General Harrison's troops attacked and destroyed Prophetstown, the largest Shawnee village. This attack, known as the Battle of Tippecanoe, left Tecumseh and his group weak. But Tecumseh did not give up.

Tecumseh and his men joined forces with the British army against the Americans at the beginning of the War of 1812. They hoped that if the British won, they would return the land to the Native Americans.

The United States fought Great Britain for control of Lake Erie during the War of 1812. In 1813, US ships won the Battle of Lake Erie, which was fought off Ohio's shores. The victory made it possible for General Harrison to cross Lake Erie into Canada in 1813. His troops defeated British and Native American forces at the Battle of the Thames. Tecumseh was killed during the fighting, and the alliance between the different Native American nations ended.

A monument to Oliver Hazard Perry (1785–1819) was built on the Ohio Island of Put-in-Bay in Lake Erie. He earned the title "Hero of Lake Erie" for leading American forces in a victory over the British in the Battle of Lake Erie during the War of 1812.

The New State Grows

After Ohio became a state, its government encouraged settlers to move into the area. Ohio grew quickly during the 1800s. By 1860, more than two million people lived in Ohio.

Commander Oliver Perry transfers to the brig *Niagara* after his flagship was damaged during the American victory in the Battle of Lake Erie in 1813.

Many Ohioans were farmers, who grew crops such as corn, beans, and melons, and raised livestock. Farmers also planted apple and peach orchards and shipped the fruit to the East Coast. They also planted tobacco. Factories were built to process Ohio's crops. Other factories began making farm equipment, such as tractors and reapers.

Improvements in transportation helped farming businesses, too. Paved roads made it easier to drive crops to the East Coast. The invention of steamboats in the early 1800s helped to deliver products quickly to the South on the Mississippi River.

Canals also helped Ohio expand its industry and transport its goods. Workers dug the long, narrow waterways so that boats could travel over hilly land. In 1832, the Ohio and Erie Canal was completed, connecting Cleveland on Lake Erie and Portsmouth on the Ohio River. In 1845, the Miami and Ohio Canal opened. It connected Toledo and Cincinnati. Although canals were important to Ohio's trade and economy, they were difficult to travel. Flooding and, during cold Ohio winters, freezing could do damage to

★ 10 KEY CITIES ★ ★ ★

Columbus

Akron

1. Columbus: population 787,033

Columbus was founded in 1812 as the state's capital. Manufacturing and steel were once key parts of Columbus's economy. Today, it has a diverse economy based on education, banking, aviation, health care, energy, and a number of other thriving industries.

2. Cleveland: population 396,815

Ohio's second most populous city is located in the northeastern portion of the state on the shores of Lake Erie. Cleveland was founded in 1796 on the Cuyahoga River. For years, the center of its economy was manufacturing.

3. Cincinnati: population 296,943

Cincinnati was the first city founded after the American Revolutionary War ended. For much of the nineteenth century, it was one of the ten largest cities by population in the United States. It is known for its beautiful architecture.

4. Toledo: population 287,208

Toledo was established in 1833. It grew and thrived quickly because of its location on the Miami and Erie Canal. Toledo has a long history of innovation in the glass industry, earning it the nickname "the Glass City."

5. Akron: population 199,110

In the early twentieth century, Akron became known as the Rubber Capital of the World because it was home to four major tire companies: Goodrich, Goodyear, Firestone, and General Tire. The city has many research and technology facilities.

OHIO

6. Dayton: population 141,527

Dayton's economy is supported by new technology companies in aerospace, defense, and other industries. Many inventors were raised in Dayton, including Orville Wright, who helped invent the airplane. Health care is another thriving industry.

7. Parma: population 81,601

Many people who work in Cleveland live in nearby Parma because of its high quality of life. In 2014, Parma was ranked as the third safest city in the nation among cities with a population of 25,000 or more.

8. Canton: population 73,007

Canton is a favorite of many football fans, as it is home to the Pro Football Hall of Fame. The organization that would become the National Football League was formed there. It is also where President William McKinley lived as an adult.

9. Youngstown: population 66,982

Youngstown's thriving coal and steel industry in the early twentieth century attracted immigrants from many places, including Italy, Greece, and what are today Lebanon, Palestine and Israel, and Syria. Today, the largest employer in the city is Youngstown State University.

10. Lorain: population 64,097

On June 28, 1924, a tornado struck the city of Lorain and nearby Sandusky. Many buildings in downtown Lorain were damaged, but the recovery process included constructing several notable buildings that still stand.

Dayton

1993   1994

KELLY

Canton

Canals were dug in Ohio in the first half of the nineteenth century to connect bodies of water and improve trade.

the canals and surrounding areas. In the northern half of the state, canals were generally drained during the winter so workers could repair any damage. The southern part of the state did not usually face the same problems. Because the canals faced so many problems, people began using other types of transportation, such as trains.

By the 1850s, railroads had become the latest improvement in transportation. Trains became a quick, cheap way to move Ohio's products throughout the country. By the 1900s, most of the canals were no longer in use.

Agriculture remained a strong industry in Ohio until the late 1800s. By then, there were more states in the Union, and Ohio farmers had trouble competing with their low prices. Many Ohioans sold their farms and moved to the cities to find other types of work. Cleveland grew into an industrial city. Cincinnati became the country's largest meatpacking center, earning it the nickname "Porkopolis."

Slavery and the Civil War

As Ohioans were getting used to life in their new state, the country faced a serious conflict between Northern states and Southern states over the issue of slavery. As a Free State, Ohio did not allow slavery. By the early 1800s, slavery was ending in the Northern states. There were millions of people still enslaved in the Southern states. Many people in Ohio were against slavery even before the Civil War. Ohio resident Harriet Beecher Stowe wrote the famous antislavery book *Uncle Tom's Cabin*, which was published in 1852.

Many enslaved people in the South tried to escape to freedom by heading to Canada. They often traveled through Ohio, where there were many abolitionists, or people who wanted to get rid of slavery. Ohioans helped formerly enslaved people escape along the Underground Railroad. This was not an actual railroad but a secret network of people and hiding places that helped fugitives from slavery travel to freedom. People who disagreed with slavery hid people who had escaped slavery in their homes. They fed, clothed, and cared for them before sending them on the next part of their journey.

The Rankin House in Ripley, Ohio, was a famous hiding place on the Underground Railroad. From 1825 to 1865, Presbyterian minister John Rankin and his wife provided shelter to more than two thousand people who had freed themselves from slavery. The home is now a museum run by the Ohio Historical Society.

After Abraham Lincoln was elected president in 1860, eleven Southern states seceded from, or left, the Union (another name for the United States at that time). Many white people in Southern states worried that their way of life was threatened because Lincoln was opposed to slavery. By the spring of 1861, the Civil War had begun. During the war, about 345,000 Ohioans fought for the North. The most famous soldier from Ohio was Ulysses S. Grant, who became the commander of the Union armies.

Ohio native Ulysses S. Grant commanded Union forces to victory in the Civil War.

Union forces defeated the South in 1865. After the war ended, the Thirteenth Amendment to the US Constitution was adopted, which outlawed slavery throughout the United States.

Political and Industrial Might

After the end of the Civil War, many people from Ohio became active in politics and industry. From 1869 to 1881, three men from Ohio became US presidents. US presidents from Ohio who served during this time included Ulysses S. Grant, Rutherford B. Hayes, and James Garfield. In

Minister John Rankin and his wife made their house a stop on the Underground Railroad for two thousand fleeing slaves.

1870, John D. Rockefeller opened the Standard Oil Company of Ohio. Within the next ten years, it owned almost all the oil refineries in the United States. In 1879, Cleveland became the first city in the country to use electric streetlights.

Construction began on Ohio's first railroad in 1835 and was completed by 1836. It connected Toledo, Ohio, to Adrian, Michigan, and covered a distance of 33 miles. The trip took three hours.

In the late 1800s, the Goodyear Tire and Rubber Company opened in Akron. The company was named after Charles Goodyear, who developed vulcanization, the process that gives

Cincinnati's Civil War Role

Cincinnati played an important role in the Civil War for several reasons. A large amount of supplies and equipment, including gunboats, armor plating, and cannons, were manufactured there. It was also a major traveling path for fugitives from slavery coming over the border from Kentucky.

rubber strength. Goodyear manufactured rubber products, such as tires, tubes, and hoses. It eventually became the country's largest tire company.

Economic Turmoil

Ohio cities were successful in the early 1900s. Tall skyscrapers and other modern office buildings were built. By the 1920s, Cleveland was the fifth-largest city in the United States.

However, in the 1930s, Ohio suffered during the **Great Depression** (1929–1939). Jobs were scarce and many people suffered greatly. Until then, Ohio had been one of the leading industrial states. It was a tough time for Ohio and the rest of the country. The US government set up programs that hired unemployed workers to build roads, dams, and other projects.

World War II

Another major event helped the economy of Ohio. World War II (1939–1945) was a global conflict, and American soldiers and their allies needed food and military equipment. The United States joined the war in 1941 after Japan bombed the US Navy base at Pearl Harbor in Hawaii. Nearly 840,000 Ohioans served in the armed forces. At home, women entered the workforce, filling jobs in factories that produced steel, weapons, and aircraft.

After the war, industries continued to grow and more people moved to the state. Cities became so crowded that developers began buying the land around the cities to build homes, and suburbs developed. At this same time, new interstate highways made it easier to travel from one major city to another. By the 1960s, Ohio was one of the most populated states.

A Time of Protests

The 1960s were also a time of turmoil for much of the country. African Americans worked for equality during the Civil Rights movement. Sometimes, however, protests turned violent in several major cities, including Cleveland.

Women joined the manufacturing workforce to help produce goods needed during World War II.

At the same time, Americans did not agree on the US being involved in the Vietnam War. Many Americans disagreed with the war. In May 1970, perhaps the most famous Vietnam War protest took place at Kent State University, near Akron. During the protest, National Guardsmen fatally shot four students and wounded nine others. The tragedy made national headlines and made more people support the antiwar movement.

Four students died when members of the National Guard fired at Vietnam War protesters on the Kent State campus.

The New Millennium and Beyond

Ohio's large industries improved the economy, but the state's factories also polluted the environment. The plants and animals in Lake Erie were dying from toxic waste being dumped into the water. Then, in 1969, a portion of the Cuyahoga River in Cleveland was so full of chemicals that it actually caught fire. Ohioans realized they had many serious environmental issues to face. Since then, Ohioans have voted to help pay for projects to improve the environment. They have been successful in many ways. In both Lake Erie and the Cuyahoga River, pollution levels have greatly decreased.

International Acclaim

In November 2015, the Ohio State University's marching band performed in London's Wembley Stadium before a National Football League game between the Buffalo Bills and Jacksonville Jaguars. They played a medley of British favorites, including songs by the Beatles, the Rolling Stones, and the Who.

The Decision

Cleveland Cavaliers star forward LeBron James made many loyal fans mad in 2010 when he announced his decision to leave the team to play for the Miami Heat. The Akron native made the announcement in a highly-viewed ESPN special called "The Decision." He returned to the Cavaliers in 2014.

During the 1980s and 1990s, new industries grew in Ohio. Computers, automobiles, paper products, and machinery became some of the most important products for the state's economy.

Today, Ohio is finding new ways to provide jobs and income for the state. By the early 2000s, many businesses had closed, while others moved to different countries. People who had worked in manufacturing jobs could no longer find work. Starting in 2007, the entire United States struggled with difficult economic times. Ohio's economy suffered, too. Now Ohioans work to bring business and money back to their state.

★10 KEY DATES IN STATE HISTORY

1. July 6, 1669

Frenchman René-Robert Cavelier, sieur de La Salle, begins his explorations of large portions of what would become the northeastern United States, including the Ohio River.

2. April 7, 1788

Marietta is established. It is the first permanent settlement by people of European descent in present-day Ohio, then part of the Northwest Territory.

3. February 19, 1803

President Thomas Jefferson signs an act of Congress to approve Ohio's boundaries and constitution. The General Assembly meets for the first time on March 1. This is the day Ohio celebrates becoming the seventeenth state.

4. July 4, 1827

The first span of the Ohio and Erie Canal is opened, stretching between Akron and Cleveland. The full canal is completed in 1832.

5. May 4, 1869

The Cincinnati Red Stockings, later the Cincinnati Reds, play their first game as the nation's first professional baseball team. The team had ten players.

6. September 7, 1963

The Pro Football Hall of Fame and Museum opens in Canton. Seventeen players are inducted the first year.

7. July 20, 1969

Neil Armstrong, born in Wapakoneta, becomes the first person to walk on the moon. An estimated six hundred million people watch the event on television.

8. September 2, 1995

The Rock and Roll Hall of Fame and Museum opens in Cleveland with a concert that includes Bob Dylan, Aretha Franklin, and others.

9. June 4, 2010

Ohio teen Anamika Veeramani wins the Scripps National Spelling Bee by correctly spelling the word "stromuhr."

10. July 21, 2015

Ohio governor John Kasich announces he is running for president in the 2016 election, becoming the sixteenth Republican to join the race. He wins the Ohio primary in April 2016.

Members of the West Side Irish American Club in Cleveland celebrate St. Patrick's Day.

The People

3

Ohio's population has grown over the past two hundred years. In 1800, just three years before Ohio officially became a state, a little more than forty-five thousand people lived there. As industries grew in Ohio, so did the population. In 1860, more than 2.4 million people lived in Ohio. By 1900, the population reached 4.2 million people. Fifty years later, close to 8 million people called Ohio home. By 2010, Ohio had just over 11.5 million residents. Today, the state population is the seventh largest in the country.

So where exactly do all these Ohioans come from? People of many different nationalities and cultures live in the Buckeye State.

Native Americans

Native Americans were the first people who lived in present-day Ohio. Scientists have enough information to guess that people lived in the area at least fifteen thousand years ago. Most of these early people were constantly moving to find food. They survived on their skills as hunters.

By the 1800s, the largest Native American groups in what is now Ohio included the Iroquois, Shawnee, Lenape, and Miami. Many of these people lived in villages near rivers and streams so they could be close to fresh water. For food, they hunted and also raised

A Native American honors his heritage at a powwow in Springfield.

crops. While people were on hunting trips, a tent called a tepee gave protection from bad weather.

As white settlers moved into the area, Native Americans found their way of life threatened. Native American nations tried to work together to protect their land and homes. Some Native Americans had to move to reservation land, or land where the government made them live. By the late 1800s, all reservations in Ohio were closed. Most Native Americans were forced to move to reservations in other states.

Today there are fewer than twenty-six thousand Native Americans in Ohio. Festivals and other gatherings give Ohio's Native Americans the chance to celebrate their history and culture.

The Europeans

The French were the first Europeans to come to the Ohio area. Most were trappers or fur traders. Many were missionaries, or people who wanted to teach the Native Americans to be Christians. After the British won the French and Indian War, they controlled the area until the American Revolution. Some former British soldiers stayed in the area. After the Revolution, many Americans of English descent began moving to Ohio.

Today, many people who live in Ohio have European ancestors. Some are descended from the early settlers. Later, people began immigrating to Ohio from throughout Europe.

During the 1840s, people from Ireland came to the United States. The Irish had depended on their potato crops, and a disease in the plants caused an event known as the Irish potato **famine**. Many Irish people starved or got sick from lack of food. Those who moved to the United States looking for work found it hard to find jobs. There was prejudice toward the Irish people, especially because of their Catholic faith. Irish immigrants often had to take tough, poorly paid jobs, such as digging Ohio's canals and laying railroad tracks. Despite these hardships, Irish immigrants and their hard work helped Ohio grow. The Irish created communities where they could hold on to their culture. Today they still celebrate their Irish heritage.

By 1850, almost half of Ohio's immigrant population came from Germany. Most Germans settled around Ohio's major cities. Some were skilled craftspeople who helped create some of Ohio's major buildings. Some cities in Ohio still have large German-American populations. For example, almost half of the people who live in Cincinnati today are descendants of German immigrants. When these German immigrants first arrived in Cincinnati, most of them lived in a neighborhood called Over-the-Rhine. German neighborhoods in the state often had German-speaking churches, clubs, and German language newspapers. Unfortunately, Germans were not always made to feel welcome in Cincinnati. In 1855, anti-German prejudice led to violence in the city.

Around 1900, many people in Ohio were of English, German, or Irish descent. By the late 1800s and early 1900s, Russians, Poles, Hungarians, Bulgarians, Croatians, Czechs, Slovaks, and people from other Eastern European areas began moving to Ohio's major cities. Immigrants from Italy and Greece also came. So many people were moving to Ohio that, in the early 1900s, almost three-fourths of Cleveland's residents said either they or their parents were born outside the United States. Like the Germans and Irish, these immigrants also faced some discrimination. Some of the people who already lived in Ohio didn't want the immigrants to practice their cultures. Luckily, the immigrants did keep many parts of their cultures and shared them with their new neighbors. They opened theater companies, newspapers, dance troupes, and other organizations. Many of the ways they shared their culture are still celebrated in Ohio today.

The Amish Community

The Amish people originally immigrated to the United States from Switzerland during the 1700s. Their beliefs were different from other Christian religions in Europe. They came to America to find religious freedom and a better life. Ohio's Holmes County, located between Columbus and Cleveland, is the home of the largest Amish community in the

★ 10 ★ KEY PEOPLE ★ ★

Neil Armstrong

Halle Berry

Tracy Chapman

1. Neil Armstrong

Born in 1930 in Wapakoneta, Armstrong was a pilot for the US Navy and later a professor of aerospace engineering. As a NASA astronaut, Armstrong became the first person to set foot on the moon, on July 20, 1969.

2. Halle Berry

In 1966, Halle Berry was born in Cleveland. In 2002, she made history as the first African-American woman to win the Academy Award for Best Actress. She is also famous for her role as Storm in the X-Men movies.

3. Drew Carey

Drew Carey was born in 1958 and raised in Cleveland. His television show *The Drew Carey Show* was set in his hometown and ran from 1995 to 2004. He also hosted *Whose Line Is It Anyway?* and *The Price is Right*.

4. Nancy Cartwright

Nancy Cartwright is a voice actor who was born in Dayton in 1957. Since 1989, she has been the voice of Bart Simpson on the Fox Network's *The Simpsons*. She also spoke the role of Chuckie on Nickelodeon's *Rugrats*.

5. Tracy Chapman

Singer Tracy Chapman was born in Cleveland in 1964. She gained fame for her 1988 single "Fast Car." Chapman has won four Grammy Awards over the course of her career, including one for another hit single, "Give Me One Reason."

6. John Legend

This singer-songwriter was born in Springfield in 1978. He has won nine Grammy Awards, one Golden Globe, and an Academy Award for his music. His 2014 single "All of Me" became one of the best-selling digital singles of all time.

7. Maya Lin

Maya Lin was born in 1959 in Athens. As a student at Yale University, she entered a national design competition for a memorial for Vietnam War veterans and won. The Vietnam Veterans Memorial in Washington, DC, was completed in 1982.

8. Annie Oakley

Born in Willowdell in 1860, Annie Oakley became known for her sharpshooting skills at the age of fifteen. She became world famous for her talent and accuracy in shooting a gun, even performing for Queen Victoria.

9. Jesse Owens

Born in 1913, Owens was eight years old when his family moved to Cleveland. He became one of the greatest track and field stars of all time. In 1976, President Gerald Ford gave Owens the Presidential Medal of Freedom.

10. Cy Young

Denton Young, born in 1867 in Gilmore, was an outstanding baseball pitcher for several professional teams. The speed and spin on his pitches earned him the nickname "Cy" for "cyclone." He won 511 games, still the Major League record.

John Legend

Maya Lin

Jesse Owens

Who Ohioans Are

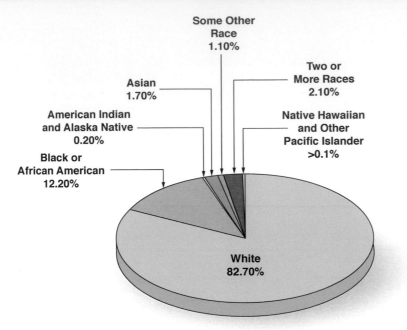

Some Other Race
1.10%

Two or More Races
2.10%

Asian
1.70%

Native Hawaiian and Other Pacific Islander
>0.1%

American Indian and Alaska Native
0.20%

Black or African American
12.20%

White
82.70%

Total Population
11,536,504

Hispanic or Latino (of any race):
• 354,674 people (3.1%)

Note: The pie chart shows the racial breakdown of the state's population based on the categories used by the US Bureau of the Census. The Census Bureau reports information for Hispanics or Latinos separately, since they may be of any race. Percentages in the pie chart may not add to 100 because of rounding.

Source: US Bureau of the Census, 2010 Census

Many Amish people work and carry on their traditions in several counties of eastern Ohio.

world. Today, nearly forty thousand Amish people live and work in these rolling hills in eastern Ohio.

Many Amish people do not believe in using modern conveniences such as electricity and automobiles. They dress plainly, practice their traditional ways of life, and live mostly off of the land. Many people travel to these areas to experience the Amish way of life. The Amish have become known for their high-quality crafts, art, and furniture. In addition to shopping for these items, visitors come to Amish country to enjoy homemade food, visit museums, and take tours of Amish historical sites.

Ohio: The Astronaut Factory

Ohio has been the home state of twenty-five astronauts, including Neil Armstrong, the first man on the moon. Over twenty-two thousand hours have been logged in space by Ohio astronauts over the course of seventy-eight space flights. Cleveland has given us the most astronauts—seven people from the city have been to space.

African Americans

In 1800, only 337 African Americans lived in Ohio, mostly in the southern part of the state. By 1860 more than 36,700 African Americans made Ohio their home. Although Ohio was a Free State, African Americans still faced prejudice. It was against the law for them to vote. Some white people in Ohio still enslaved African American people, even though it was against the law.

After the Civil War, many African Americans moved to Ohio's cities to find work. Life in the city was not easy for black workers, and jobs that paid well were hard to find. Many African Americans worked in factories during this time. Others worked as day laborers, nannies, or housekeepers. Some worked in restaurants. Because they feared violence and racism, most black Ohioans lived in their own communities. Black people could not vote, serve on juries, or send their children to public school. Even in the 1900s, when these laws no longer existed, there was still racism against black people in Ohio. In the early 1900s, Ohio's African-American population continued to grow as more people moved from the Southern United States to the North in search of work or a better life for their families. In 1959, the state passed the Ohio Civil Rights Act, which helped stop discrimination against African Americans.

Today's black Ohioans have succeeded in various fields. Some important African Americans from Ohio include Pulitzer Prize winner Rita Dove, who in 1993 became the first African American—and the youngest person—to be named poet laureate of the United States. Also in 1993, Ohioan Toni Morrison became the first African American to receive the Nobel Prize in Literature.

Today, more than 1.4 million African Americans live in the state. They represent around 12 percent of Ohio's population.

Other Cultures

Hispanic Americans and Asian Americans make up the next largest minorities in Ohio. Few Hispanics lived in Ohio until the 1960s. At that time, Latinos began immigrating to the United States from Central and South American countries, Mexico, and the Caribbean in search of jobs. According to the 2010 US Census (a tool used to count the people living in the US), more than 35,000 Hispanic Americans live in Ohio. They are about 3.1 percent of the state's population.

According to the 2014 census, Asians are the fastest growing racial group in Ohio. In 2014, about 2.0 percent of people living in Ohio were of Asian descent. They trace their ancestries to China, Japan, India, Korea, the Philippines, Vietnam, and other Asian countries. One reason for the increase of Asian Americans in Ohio might be that Ohio companies are doing more business with Asian companies. There are also many medical and technical jobs that pay well and require high levels of education. Immigrants who have education and experience can find jobs there. Ohio also has many colleges and universities, so students come from other countries to study there.

Writer Toni Morrison, born in Lorain, achieved a milestone when she received the Nobel Prize in Literature.

Education

Education has always been important to Ohioans. Early settlers built one-room schoolhouses made of logs. Before there were public schools in Ohio, parents paid or traded goods for their children to go to school. In 1853, the state's first public high schools opened their doors.

Founded in 1833, Ohio's Oberlin College was the first US college to admit women. It was also one of the country's first colleges to admit African Americans. The college was a key stop on the Underground Railroad. In 1858, a group of people who lived in Oberlin and a nearby town called Wellington rescued a fugitive from slavery named John Price and took him to Canada. The rescuers were sent to jail for helping, but they were later released. The

Students take part in an event at Cleveland State University, one of many colleges in Ohio.

case was known as the Oberlin-Wellington Rescue. Newspapers across the US printed the story. Some historians believe this case was important to the start of the Civil War.

Today, Ohio is home to many well-respected colleges and universities. In 1862, the Morrill Act was passed. This law allowed states to sell large areas of land donated by the federal government in order to raise money to build public colleges. Thanks to this act, the college that is now the Ohio State University, also called Ohio State, was established in Columbus in 1870. Its first class had just twenty-four students. Today, Ohio State has nearly sixty thousand students and is one of the country's largest universities. Other public and private colleges and universities include Ohio University, Miami University, Oberlin College, Case Western Reserve University, Denison University, Baldwin Wallace University, Bowling Green State University, and Ohio Wesleyan University.

All-American Soap Box Derby

All Horse Parade

1. All-American Soap Box Derby

Each July, Akron hosts the All-American Soap Box Derby, a racing program in which kids ages seven to twenty drive homemade, engineless cars down an incline. The "Greatest Amateur Racing Event in the World" attracts racers from everywhere.

2. All Horse Parade

This September parade in Delaware kicks off the Delaware County Fair. Hundreds of horses are part of the parade, as well as vintage horse-drawn wagons, sleighs, and fire engines. Marching bands join the parade as well.

3. Americana Festival

Over seventy thousand people celebrate Independence Day in Centerville at the Americana Festival. A street fair, 5K race, and an arts and crafts exhibit are part of the fun, as well as many children's activities, including pony rides and a petting zoo.

4. Fabulous 50s Fling and Car Show

This June festival in Sugarcreek provides a chance to view classic automobiles, custom cars, and hot rods. The weekend includes car competitions, a 5K race, live music, and homemade food for sale. The festival has been held since 1991.

5. Festival Latino

Each August, Columbus residents celebrate the heritage of their Latin American community at the largest festival of its kind in Ohio. Traditional music is featured, as well as dance lessons, food, and arts and crafts.

OHIO

6. Gourmet Food Truck Competition and Rally

The Gourmet Food Truck Competition and Rally brings dozens
of food trucks to the Miami County Fairgrounds in Troy
each May. Approximately ten thousand people attend the
competition to sample food and raise funds for the fair.

7. Johnny Appleseed Festival

In late September, Lisbon hosts this festival to celebrate a
beloved fall fruit: the apple. Attendees can enjoy all kinds of
homemade products, including apple butter, apple fritters,
apple dumplings, and apple pie. Activities include a parade,
music, and more.

8. Ohio State Fair

More than eight hundred thousand people attend the annual
Ohio State Fair, held in Columbus in early August. For more
than 150 years, the fair has celebrated Ohio's products,
people, and history.

9. Vectren Dayton Air Show

The Dayton Air Show is considered one of the country's top
aviation events. The show, held each July, takes place at
Dayton International Airport. Visitors can climb aboard
some of the historic featured aircraft.

10. Window Wonderland

Window Wonderland is a holiday festival held in Wooster
each November. Storefront windows are decorated with
old-fashioned charm and holiday art. Attendees can enjoy
a Christmas tree lighting and free hot cocoa and cookies.

Ohio State Fair

Vectren Dayton Air Show

The building with the green cupola is a replica
of the original state capitol in Chillicothe.

How the Government Works

4

Ohio's constitution was created in 1802, one year before Ohio became a part of the Union. According to the constitution, the state government must be divided into three branches, or sections: the executive branch, the legislative branch, and the judicial branch. The executive branch administers state laws, the legislative branch makes laws, and the judicial branch enforces and interprets laws. The state government is centered in the state capital, Columbus. This was not always the case, though. When Ohio first became a state in 1803, the capital was Chillicothe. It was later moved to Zanesville. Community leaders and politicians in Ohio continued to fight about where the capital should be. Finally, they decided to move the capital to the middle of the state, so Columbus was chosen.

Each of Ohio's eighty-eight counties, as well as each village and city, has a local government. Most counties have a board of commissioners who are elected. Many of Ohio's cities elect a mayor who enforces local laws and manages the city government's budget. If a town has five thousand or more people in it according to the most recent US census, it is considered a city. If it has less than that, it is considered a village.

Taxes help pay for state and local governments. Residents often have to pay property, income, and sales taxes. Property taxes are based on the value of a person's home or

A statue of Christopher Columbus stands outside City Hall in the city that bears his name.

Cleveland Boosters

In the early 1980s, Cleveland mayor George Voinovich led a campaign to improve Cleveland's public image. The campaign's slogan was "New York's the Big Apple, but Cleveland's a plum." Voinovich even used a plum to throw out the first pitch at a game between the New York Yankees and the Cleveland Indians.

other personal possessions, such as an automobile. When people buy certain products at a store, they pay a sales tax that might go partly to the state government and partly to the local government. State and other income taxes are taken out of a worker's paycheck or paid directly by people who are self-employed. State and local taxes help pay for schools, police and fire departments, and public libraries. They also pay for town and state buildings and government services such as snow removal and lifeguards for public pools.

Ohio is often called the Mother of US Presidents. Seven presidents were born in Ohio: Ulysses S. Grant, Rutherford B. Hayes, James Garfield, Benjamin Harrison, William McKinley, William Howard Taft, and Warren G. Harding. William Henry Harrison was born in Virginia but lived in Ohio when he ran for president.

Ohio is considered an important state during US presidential elections. Usually, the presidential candidate that wins in Ohio also wins for the country. In fact, no Republican

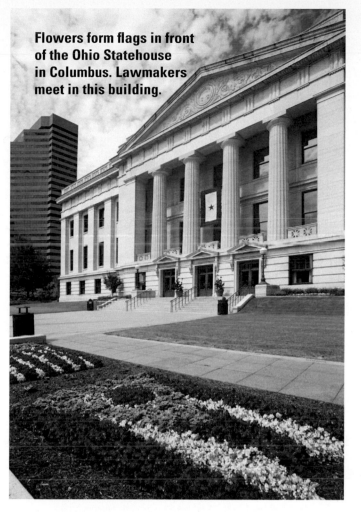
Flowers form flags in front of the Ohio Statehouse in Columbus. Lawmakers meet in this building.

has ever won the presidency without winning Ohio's electoral votes. The population is close to evenly split between Democrats and Republicans, and the state's electoral votes have been important to the election many times before.

Branches of Government

Executive

The governor is the head of the executive branch. The governor is responsible for managing a state budget, signing bills that are passed in the legislature, and choosing the directors of state departments and agencies. The governor is elected to a four-year term. He or she can serve only two terms in a row.

Legislative

Ohio's legislature is called the Ohio General Assembly. It has two houses, or chambers: the house of representatives and the senate. The General Assembly has grown with Ohio. The first meeting of the general assembly was in March of 1803. At that time, there were only thirty state representatives and fourteen members of the senate. Now Ohio has ninety-nine state representatives and thirty-three members of the senate. State senators may serve no more than two four-year terms. State representatives may serve no more than four two-year terms. The main role of state representatives and senators is to debate and vote on proposed laws (bills). If the general assembly votes in favor of a bill, the governor may sign it into law.

Judicial

This branch is made up of the Ohio Supreme Court and many lower courts, including courts of appeals, courts of common pleas, county courts, municipal courts, and the court of claims. The main job of the state supreme court justices (judges) is to rule on cases that can't be agreed on in a lower court. State supreme court justices can decide whether or not a state law agrees with the state constitution. They also review all death penalty cases. One chief justice and six justices sit on the supreme court. They can be elected to an unlimited number of six-year terms.

Representation in Washington, DC

Like all Americans, the people of Ohio are represented in the US Congress in Washington, DC. Each state elects two US senators, who serve six-year terms. There is no limit on the number of terms a US senator can serve. The number of people living in a state determines the number of people it can send to the US House of Representatives. After the 2010 census, Ohio was allowed sixteen representatives in the House. They can be elected to an unlimited number of two-year terms.

John Glenn was the first American to orbit the Earth, and he represented Ohio in the US Senate for twenty-five years.

Ohio has had many representatives in the federal government, but John Glenn Jr. is unique. Glenn was born on July 18, 1921, in Cambridge, Ohio. In 1962, he became the first American astronaut to orbit Earth. After retiring as an astronaut, he represented Ohio as a US senator from 1974 to 1999. In 1998, at age seventy-seven, he returned to space, becoming the oldest person to travel outside Earth's atmosphere.

How a Bill Becomes a Law

Members of the Ohio house and senate may either create new laws or change old ones. A law begins as a bill, which can be proposed by either a state senator or a state representative. Ideas for bills can come from any Ohio citizen. Anyone who lives in Ohio and has an idea for a new law can present it to their representative or senator.

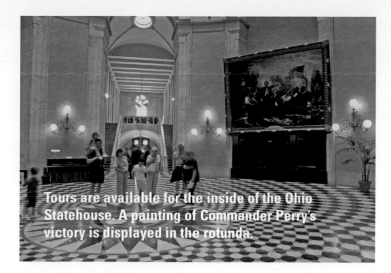
Tours are available for the inside of the Ohio Statehouse. A painting of Commander Perry's victory is displayed in the rotunda.

In the legislature, a representative's or senator's proposal for a bill is written in legal language, recorded, and then considered. A bill introduced by a representative is first considered in the house, and a bill introduced by a senator is first considered in the senate.

First, the bill is debated by a committee. The committee might allow individuals and groups to talk about why they do or do not want the bill to become a law. If the committee approves the bill, it is next debated in the full house or senate. If the members of that chamber pass the bill, it goes to the other chamber. The same process gets repeated there.

Once both chambers have approved a bill in exactly the same form, it is sent to the governor for his or her signature. If the governor signs the bill (or takes no action on it for ten days), it becomes a law. However, the governor may also veto, or reject, the bill if he or she does not agree with it. If that happens, the bill might die. It can still become a law if both houses vote on it.

In Their Own Words

"If Ohio is not a member of the Union and we have some illegal members of the Senate and the House here, I should like to know it."
—Representative John Lyle of Texas, jokingly, on the day Ohio's constitution was officially ratified in 1953

POLITICAL FIGURES
FROM OHIO

★ Nickie Antonio: Ohio State Senate 2019-

A native of Lakewood, Antonio represented the thirteenth district in the Ohio House of Representatives, an area located in Cuyahoga County. She is a former member of the Lakewood City Council, a role she served in from 2005 to 2010. She began serving in the senate in 2019.

★ Ulysses S. Grant: US President, 1869-1877

Born in Point Pleasant in 1822, Ulysses S. Grant served as the eighteenth president of the United States. During the Civil War, Grant was one of the most successful Union generals, and he rose to become commander of all Union forces. He is buried in New York City, in the largest tomb in North America.

★ John Kasich: Governor, 2011-2019

Kasich has been a resident of Ohio since he attended college at Ohio State University. In addition to serving as governor, he also represented Ohio's twelfth district in the US House of Representatives and, before that, in Ohio's state senate. He ran for the Republican nomination in the 2016 presidential election.

OHIO

Contacting Lawmakers

Ohioans can take an active role in government and contact their representative and senator about issues of concern. Legislators are there to serve Ohioans and the state. To contact Ohio state legislators, go to:

www.legislature.state.oh.us

Enter your zip code or district number to find your senator or representative.

Your representatives in the US Congress are advocating for you on national matters. To contact your representative in Congress, go to:

www.house.gov/representatives/find

Enter your zip code to find contact information for your representative in Congress.

Cell Phone Use in Cars Restricted

Using a cell phone while driving a car is a dangerous habit, and one that leads to many accidents and injuries every year. Several states have passed laws banning texting while driving. Ohio became one of the latest to pass such a law in 2012, and citizens and advocacy groups played a role in helping the bill get passed.

The origins of the law can be traced back to 1999, when the city of Brooklyn, Ohio, banned cell phone usage behind the wheel. Since then, concerned citizens, law enforcement officials, and groups that promote safe driving have communicated with their representatives to ask for greater and more widespread regulation of texting while driving. In 2012, these efforts paid off when the Ohio House of Representatives passed House Bill 99, the law that banned hand-held cell phone usage while driving (hands-free devices may be used by adults). Governor John Kasich signed the bill in June 2012, and in August of that year, the statewide ban went into effect. The law also had additional specific regulations related to using a cell phone while driving. For people under age eighteen, using a cell phone in any way while driving is prohibited. For all Ohio residents, writing, reading, or sending texts, e-mails or any text-based communication is against the law.

Apples have been an important crop in Ohio since Johnny Appleseed, whose real name was John Chapman, planted his first orchards in the early nineteenth century.

Making a Living

The two main industries in Ohio are agriculture (farming) and manufacturing. Since the first settlers in Ohio planted and cultivated seeds, agriculture has helped Ohioans make a living. Today, Ohio's farm products are used throughout the state. They are also exported to other states and countries.

Agriculture

Agriculture has gone through both good and bad times since Ohio became a state. The Great Depression hit Ohio farmers at the same time as a very long drought that caused crops to die. World War II, on the other hand, meant that more food was needed, which helped Ohio farmers. However, from 1950-1999, there were fewer and fewer farms in Ohio. The cost of food fell while the cost of living increased. Farmers were getting less for their crops at the same time that they were paying more for clothing, electricity, and machinery. In time, many people sold their farms and moved to the cities.

Ohio still has about eighty thousand farms, which cover about half the state. The major crops include soybeans, corn, hay, oats, and wheat. Most of these grains are fed to cattle. Ohio's cattle provide milk and beef. Ohio also is a major producer of hogs, ranks very high in the production of eggs, and makes more Swiss cheese than any other state.

Johnny Appleseed helped feed many of Ohio's first settlers with apples from his orchards.

Corn—one of Ohio's largest crops—is grown throughout the state. It is Ohio's second-most-valuable crop, after soybeans. Ohio is one of the top ten corn-producing states in the country. Most of this corn is not eaten by people, though. More than half goes to feeding livestock, such as cows. Corn is also used to make a variety of products, from plastic and ethanol (a type of fuel) to cereal, cooking oil, glue, and ink.

Apples are another important state product. Ohioans are very proud of their famous apple farmer, John Chapman (1774–1845), known as Johnny Appleseed. Legend says that when Ohio became a state, Johnny Appleseed was traveling all over the region, planting apple orchards. Some of those trees, now two hundred years old, continue to bear fruit. The Johnny Appleseed Educational Center and Museum on the campus of Urbana University in Urbana honors this legend. Outside the museum are apple trees that started as cuttings from trees planted by Johnny Appleseed.

Ohio farmers also produce grapes and strawberries. Vegetables such as cucumbers and tomatoes are major crops in Ohio as well. Ohio farmers rank tenth in the United States for growing strawberries. More than 710 acres of farmland are used just for strawberries. About 3 million pounds of strawberries were grown in 2009. Strawberries are sometimes hard to grow, but Ohio's university researchers are working to find new types of strawberries to help farmers in Ohio grow more of this tasty fruit.

Manufacturing

Manufacturing is also important to Ohio's economy. Ohio is a leading manufacturer of cars, trucks, motor vehicle parts, jet engines, airplane parts, and other transportation equipment. Some Ohioans work in factories that produce steel and tools. Ohio is one of the top steel-producing states in the country.

Ohio has many different kinds of factories. The city of Napoleon, for example, is home to the world's largest soup factory. Wellston is the world's leading maker of frozen pizzas.

Cincinnati has the biggest soap factory in the United States. Other major products made in Ohio include computer parts, rubber, electrical equipment, clay, glass, and paper and plastic items. Toledo is known as "the Glass City" because it has a long history of creating and manufacturing glass products. Windows, bottles, windshields, and even glass art have been produced in Toledo. Several large glass companies were founded there, including Owens Corning, Libbey Glass, Pilkington North America, and Therma-Tru.

Many food-processing plants in Ohio handle the products that are grown on Ohio's farms. Some types of food-processing plants include those that pack meat, preserve and can fruits, and make dairy products.

Some Ohio manufacturers build high-tech products. **Biotechnology** companies use items found in nature to make their products. Many of these companies are opening or growing in Ohio. The products they make could help cure diseases, create new energy sources, or support scientific research.

Mining

Mining also helps the state's economy. Ohio is one of the country's top coal-mining states. Coal is the state's most valuable mineral. For a long time, coal mining had no laws set by the state, and many coal miners worked in dangerous conditions. The mines were harmful to the surrounding soil and environment. In 1947, Ohio passed the Strip Coal Mining Act. This helped make coal mining safer and less harmful to the environment around mines.

Coal mining continues to be an important industry in Ohio. All of the coal is mined in eighteen counties in the eastern part of the state.

★ 10 KEY ★ INDUSTRIES

Automobiles

Biosciences

1. Advanced Energy

Advanced energy is a growing source of jobs in Ohio. These companies make new, more efficient ways of creating or harnessing the energy we use in our everyday lives—for example, fuel cells that power electric cars.

2. Aerospace and Aviation

Ohio is called the birthplace of aviation because it is the birthplace of Orville Wright, one of the inventors of the powered airplane. Today, the state is where new flight-related technology is researched, developed, and manufactured.

3. Automobiles

Automobile manufacturing is a $19.3 billion annual industry in the state. That is about 13 percent of total US output. Ohio is the second-largest producer of motor vehicles in the United States, after Michigan.

4. Banking

The financial services industry is one of Ohio's most important sectors. This industry includes commercial banks, financial advisor firms, credit card companies, and mortgage companies. The northeast region of the state is home to most of these jobs.

5. Biosciences

Bioscience, also known as life science, deals with living organisms or naturally-found matter to improve the lives of humans. The state's many universities and research facilities make Ohio an ideal location for more than two thousand bioscience firms.

6. Coal

Coal is Ohio's most important mined resource. The coal is mined in the eastern part of the state. Although miners have been digging for a long time, scientists believe more than 20 billion tons (18 billion metric tons) of coal remain.

7. Electronics

Instruments, controls, and electronics are an important part of the Ohio economy. In 2014, Ohio ranked fourth in the nation in employment in electrical equipment manufacturing. Many other companies in Ohio use these electronics, like car manufacturers.

8. Food Processing

A large number of skilled workers, access to materials suppliers, and plenty of fresh water from Lake Erie have helped Ohio's food processing industry thrive. The state is also home to many food-related research centers that help support these companies.

9. Salt

Ohio is home to large deposits of salt about 2,000 feet (600 m) underground. Ohio is one of the country's largest producers of rock salt, which is used to melt snow. The state mines about 4 million tons (3.6 million t) each year.

10. Soybeans

Although most of the state's soybeans are fed to cattle, some are used to make a nondairy substitute for milk. Soybeans are used in nonfood items such as hand cleaners, chemical cleaners, and lubricants that help machines run smoothly.

Food Processing

Salt

Recipe for Apple Chips

Apples are one of Ohio's tastiest and most nutritious crops. Choose your favorite kind of apple to make these apple chips. They're a healthy way to enjoy a sweet snack.

What You Need

2 cups (0.47 liters) unsweetened apple juice

1 cinnamon stick

2 whole apples

What To Do

- Ask an adult for help with the oven and stove. Heat oven to 250°F (120°C).
- Place the cinnamon stick and apple juice in a pot on the stove and bring to a low boil.
- Slice about 0.5 inches (1.3 cm) off the top and bottom of both apples. Use an apple corer or knife to remove the core.
- Slice each apple into very thin pieces crosswise (so you end up with circular pieces).
- Put the apple pieces into the boiling juice for four to five minutes.
- Remove the apples from the juice and pat dry with paper towels.
- Lay the chips on a baking sheet in a single layer. Make sure none of the pieces are touching.
- Bake 30 to 40 minutes. Apples should be brown and almost dry when finished.
- Turn off the oven. Let chips cool completely before removing from oven.

Plastic Pioneers

The five-county area around Akron has long been known as "Polymer Valley" because of the region's success in the research, development, and production of plastic. However, polymer companies are scattered throughout the state, and recently a concentration of these manufacturers has sprung up in southeastern Ohio as well.

Oil, natural gas, salt, clay, sandstone, and other minerals are also mined in Ohio. Sandstone and other minerals are used to construct buildings and highways. Many of these materials are also important to other Ohio industries, such as steel and glass manufacturing. Mining is not as important to Ohio's economy as it was in the past. However, it still earns a lot of money for the state. In 2014, Ohio's coal and industrial minerals were worth $2.18 billion.

The Business of Service

Most workers in Ohio have jobs in the service industry. This industry includes banking, health care, education, restaurants, retail stores, and hotels.

Tourism is a major part of the state's service industry as well. Each year, millions of people visit Ohio. Tourists relax on Ohio's lakeshore, hike through its parks, or visit the state's many historic sites and museums. Others enjoy the different festivals, fairs, and other events in Ohio's cities and towns. All these people spend money in the state. That money makes a profit for many service businesses. When tourists buy things, they also pay taxes which go to state and local governments. The tourism industry also employs many Ohioans, including tour guides, museum curators, hotel clerks, waitstaff, and store clerks.

Tourist Attractions

Tourists visiting Ohio have plenty to keep them busy. Ohio has many exciting historical, cultural, and recreational attractions. Tourists flock to Cedar Point amusement park in Sandusky in northern Ohio. Officially called "The Roller Coaster Capital of the World," Cedar Point holds the world record for the most roller coasters in one park—seventeen in all. Cedar Point has more rides than any other amusement park in the world.

Zoos are another state attraction. The Cincinnati Zoo and Botanical Garden is the second-oldest zoo in the United States. Animal lovers can also visit zoos in Columbus, Toledo, and Cleveland.

Cedar Point, which opened in Sandusky in 1870, has more roller coasters than any other amusement park in the world.

Medical Leader

Ohio's Cleveland Clinic is known around the world for its high success rates in treating many kinds of diseases, especially heart problems. Its main campus consists of forty-one buildings, and it operates fourteen other health centers in the Cleveland community. Cleveland Clinic also has facilities in Florida, Nevada, Canada, and Abu Dhabi, UAE.

Ohio is home to several "halls of fame." The Rock and Roll Hall of Fame and Museum, located on Lake Erie in downtown Cleveland, opened in 1995. The museum is inside a giant glass pyramid. More than 7.5 million people visit it each year. Visitors learn about the histories of their favorite rock stars and get an up-close look at music memorabilia. Sports fans and motorcycle enthusiasts can head to Canton's Pro Football Hall of Fame or the Motorcycle Hall of Fame Museum in Pickerington.

Historic Ohio draws tourists of all ages. The state honors some of its flight pioneers with the Armstrong Air and Space Museum in Wapakoneta and the National Museum of the US Air Force in Dayton. The Air Force museum includes exhibits on the Wright brothers.

Other famous Ohio natives have museums in their honor. Tourists can visit the Thomas Edison Birthplace Museum in Milan and learn about the inventor of the light

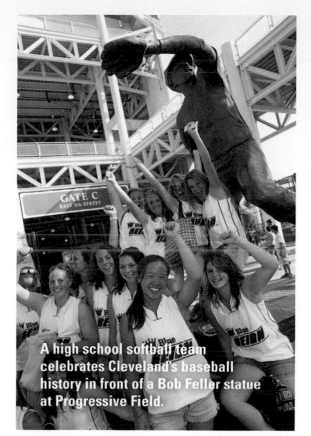
A high school softball team celebrates Cleveland's baseball history in front of a Bob Feller statue at Progressive Field.

bulb, the record player, and the motion-picture camera. Jack Nicklaus, one of history's greatest golfers, is honored at the Jack Nicklaus Museum in Columbus, his hometown.

Science buffs can visit the Goodyear World of Rubber in Akron or the Toledo Center of Science and Industry. Nature lovers can enjoy underground caves at Seneca Caverns in Bellevue or waterfalls and hiking at Wayne National Forest or Hocking Hills State Park in southeastern Ohio.

Professional sports provide enjoyment for Ohio residents and visitors. Ohio has teams in all four major professional sports leagues. Columbus has hockey's Blue Jackets. Cincinnati is home to baseball's Reds and football's Bengals. Cleveland has baseball's Indians, basketball's Cavaliers, and football's Browns. Columbus is also home to the Crew of Major League Soccer. The team plays at Mapfre Stadium, the first soccer-specific stadium in the United States.

The Ohio State University competes in more than two dozen varsity sports and has one of the top-ranked football teams in the country. The Buckeyes play in the state's largest stadium.

The Future

The people of Ohio want to protect their environment, but they also want their economy to grow. More businesses might mean more jobs and money, but do they also mean more pollution and damage to the environment? Developing high-technology and other "clean" industries may help the people of Ohio have a strong economy and still keep their state clean and beautiful.

OHIO ★ ★ ★ ★ ★
STATE MAP

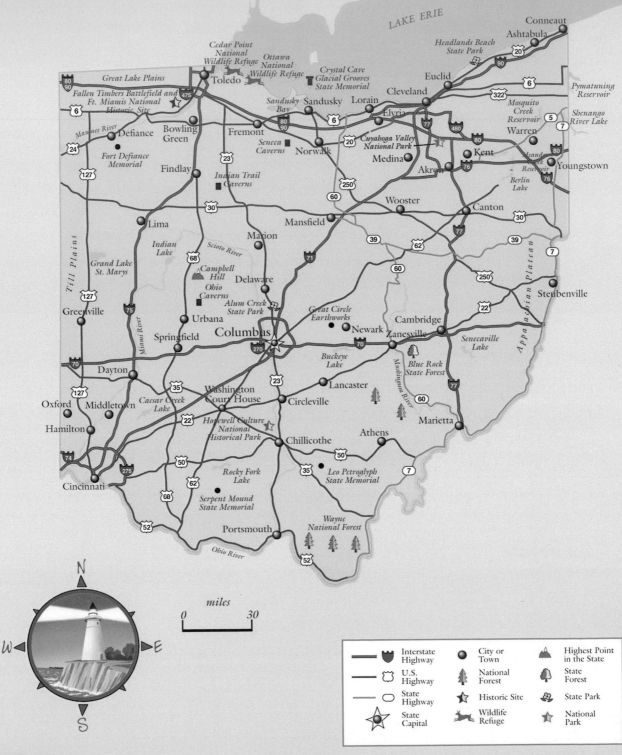

LAKE ERIE

Conneaut
Ashtabula
Headlands Beach State Park
Cedar Point National Wildlife Refuge
Ottawa National Wildlife Refuge
Crystal Cave Glacial Grooves State Memorial
Great Lake Plains
Toledo
Euclid
Cleveland
Pymatuning Reservoir
Fallen Timbers Battlefield and Ft. Miamis National Historic Site
Sandusky Bay
Sandusky
Lorain
Elyria
Mosquito Creek Reservoir
Shenango River Lake
Defiance
Bowling Green
Fremont
Cuyahoga Valley National Park
Warren
Maumee River
Fort Defiance Memorial
Seneca Caverns
Norwalk
Medina
Akron
Kent
Berlin Lake
Youngstown
Findlay
Indian Trail Caverns
Wooster
Canton
Lima
Mansfield
Indian Lake
Scioto River
Marion
Grand Lake St. Marys
Campbell Hill
Ohio Caverns
Delaware
Steubenville
Greenville
Alum Creek State Park
Urbana
Columbus
Great Circle Earthworks
Newark
Zanesville
Senecaville Lake
Appalachian Plateau
Springfield
Buckeye Lake
Blue Rock State Forest
Muskingum River
Dayton
Washington Court House
Lancaster
Marietta
Oxford
Middletown
Caesar Creek Lake
Circleville
Athens
Hamilton
Hopewell Culture National Historical Park
Chillicothe
Leo Petroglyph State Memorial
Cincinnati
Rocky Fork Lake
Serpent Mound State Memorial
Wayne National Forest
Portsmouth
Ohio River
Till Plains
Miami River

N
W   E
S

miles
0   30

Legend
—	Interstate Highway
—	U.S. Highway
—	State Highway
★	State Capital
●	City or Town
🌲	National Forest
★	Historic Site
🦌	Wildlife Refuge
⛰	Highest Point in the State
🌳	State Forest
State Park
★	National Park

OHIO
MAP SKILLS

1. The city of Newark is located near which interstate highway?

2. Which city is located at the most northeastern point of the state?

3. If you were in Urbana and traveled south on US Highway 68, what city would you reach first?

4. What direction should you travel from Chillicothe in order to reach Wayne National Forest?

5. Which state park is located closest to Ohio's capital city?

6. What is the name of the river closest to Cincinnati?

7. If you traveled east on US Highway 6 from Bowling Green, which city would you reach first?

8. Which lake is located southwest of Newark?

9. How many cities are located on or very near to US Highway 23 in Ohio?

10. Which body of water is located east of Middletown?

Interstate 70

Springfield

10. Caesar Creek Lake

9. Six: Marion, Delaware, Columbus, Circleville, Chillicothe, and Portsmouth.

8. Buckeye Lake

7. Fremont

6. Ohio River

5. Alum Creek State Park

4. Southeast

3. Springfield

2. Conneaut

1. Interstate 70.

State Flag, Seal, and Song

Ohio's flag is shaped like a pennant with red and white stripes and a large blue triangle. The triangle has seventeen white stars in it. The thirteen stars grouped around the circle represent the thirteen original colonies. The other four white stars near the corner of the triangle symbolize Ohio becoming the seventeenth state. The white "O" stands for "Ohio," and the red center symbolizes the buckeye. The blue triangle represents the state's hills and valleys. The red and white stripes stand for Ohio's roads and waterways.

The Ohio state seal depicts a rising sun with thirteen rays, representing the original colonies. The sun is rising over Mount Logan. In the middle ground is the Scioto River. There is also a bundle of wheat, which stands for Ohio's agriculture and bounty. Next to the wheat is a bundle of seventeen arrows, which refer to Ohio's being the seventeenth state to join the Union.

A song called "Beautiful Ohio" became the state's official song in 1969. The lyrics were written by Ballard McDonald and the music by Mary Earl. View the song's lyrics at: **www.50states.com/songs/ohio**.

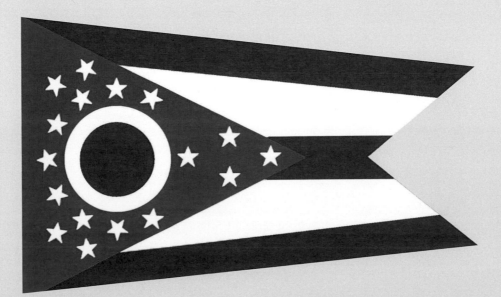

Glossary

beach ridges Sandy deposits that rise above the otherwise flat ground.

biotechnology The science of using living or naturally occurring things to create new products that improve lives.

breechcloth A traditional Native American cloth garment worn around the hips, usually by men.

decimated When a large part of a population, either human, animal, or plant, is killed or destroyed. This can also refer to cities or areas.

endangered When an animal or plant species is harmed or destroyed and in danger of extinction.

flint A very hard, fine-grained mineral that has sharp edges and throws off a spark when struck with steel.

Great Depression A time of declining economic activity in the worldwide economy from the late 1920s through the 1930s.

horticulture The science of growing plants, including fruits, vegetables, and decorative varieties such as flowers.

induct To admit as a member or ceremonially install in a position or office.

ratified Confirmed by agreeing to or giving approval.

US Census Bureau A government agency responsible for gathering and producing data about the American people.

More About Ohio

BOOKS

Jerome, Kate Boehm. *Ohio: What's So Great About This State?* Mount Pleasant, SC: Arcadia Publishing, 2010.

Kurtz, Jane. *Celebrating Ohio.* 50 States to Celebrate. Boston: Houghton Mifflin Harcourt, 2015.

Marsh, Carole. *Ohio Native Americans.* Peachtree City, GA: Gallopade International, 2004.

Schonberg, Marcia. *Ohio History.* Portsmouth, NH: Heinemann, 2009.

WEBSITES

The Official State Website—Kids Page
ohio.gov/government/kids

The Ohio Digital Library—Kids Section
ohioebooks.org/kids

Ohio History Connection
www.ohiohistory.org

ABOUT THE AUTHORS

Joyce Hart is a native of Ohio who graduated from the University of Oregon and raised her children in Eugene. A freelance author and editor, she enjoys traveling the backroads of the Pacific Northwest.

Lisa M. Herrington is a children's writer and editor who has extensive family in the Cleveland and Youngstown areas. She enjoys visiting the shores of Lake Erie. She lives in Trumbull, Connecticut, with her husband and daughter.

Kerry Jones Waring is a writer and editor from Buffalo, New York, where she lives with her husband and son.

Index

Page numbers in **boldface** are illustrations. Entries in **boldface** are glossary terms.

Index